Out Of The Darkness Of Depression

Positive Strategies To Guide You

Allan G. Hedberg, Ph.D.

Serendipity Media Group, LLC.
http://www.serendipitymediagroup.com

TABLE OF CONTENTS

ACKNOWLEDGMENTS

The author would like to acknowledge Dr. Hap LaCrone and Dr. Eugene Walker for encouraging me to write the first edition of the book, *DEPRESSION: POSITIVE STRATEGIES FOR CHANGE.* By doing so they had a part of impacting the lives of many individuals who drew strength and guidance from the first edition of this book.

I also thank my wife, Bernice, who offered ongoing guidance and help in the writing and formatting the book. She always desires my books to be books with the greatest impact on the greatest number of people.

Thanks goes to the staff of Serendipity Media Group, especially Gina Meyers, who guided the publication process of this 2nd edition to its final destination, the hands and lives of the readers who deal with some form of depression in their lives every day.

Special thanks to Rob Carey, an internationally acclaimed artist, who sketched the tree on the cover from location in Wollbach, Germany.

Allan G. Hedberg, Ph.D.

DEDICATION

It is an honor to dedicate this book, which addresses a problem that 20% of the population experience, to six people who were my primary encouragers at the time I was deciding my college major and my life's career – my father, my wife, Dr. Edith Grotberg, Dr. "Woody" Woodward, Dr. John Knowles, and Dr. Arthur Arthur.

PREFACE

Books are written for different purposes and for different readers. This book was designed to serve as a manual for those who seek to better manage and overcome depression. It provides a basic understanding of the nature of depression and will prove to be a valuable resource for those who are concerned about preventing depression and treating it. Positive strategies for the personal management of depression are emphasized throughout the book.

The following three groups of individuals were focused upon as this manuscript was prepared:

1. Individuals who personally experience the painful effects of depression, but can learn to control circumstances in their lives and thereby come to live more effectively and victoriously over depression.

2. Family and friends of depressed individuals who desire to learn how best to relate to their depressed family member or friend and how to be a constructive and nondepressing influence.

3. Professional therapists who are consulted by depressed individuals and their families for support and specific guidance to bring about desired change.

Depression is the result of having learned a destructive pattern of self-defeating behavior. Hence, self control can be learned as one of the basic components to the management of depression. The alternative to depression can be learned as well, but it may require psychotherapy and the consistent supportive involvement from a wide variety of friendly individuals.

CHAPTER I

THE BASICS OF DEPRESSION

Reflections of the Times in Which We Live

The gray cloak of depression weighs heavily upon the lives of millions of Americans. It is a costly garb, whether it is measured in terms of human suffering or in terms of dollars. The suffering is not only experienced by depressed individuals but also by those close to them. It is estimated that 50 to 100 people out of every thousand experience the painful pall of depression in a significant way and warrant treatment at sometime in their life. The range of individuals who experience serious depression is between 10% and 15% of the total population. Seventy-five percent of all psychiatric hospitalizations are related to depression, according to a report produced by the National Institute of Mental Health in 1973. The dollar cost of depression at that time was established to fall just under 10 billion dollars annually. In today's economy it would greatly exceed that cost. The business world suffers from this serious malady. It appears that there is at least a 20% to 25% loss of efficiency during the work day by employees because of distractions associated with significant depression. Although depression is a reflection of our times, it is not a new malady. Professionals have been attempting to understand depression since the days of Hypocrites.

Dr. Martin Seligman, psychologist, characterized depression as the "common cold" of psychopathology. Like most common colds, depression runs its own course in time. Most suffer depression in the wake of some particular traumatic event such as the death of a close loved-one, the break up of a love relationship, a serious chronic illness or injury, job failure, or the unexplained rejection of a friend. Most of us recover from such experiences without becoming significantly disabled or requiring psychotherapy. However, others succumb or give up under such circumstances and become like T.S. Eliot's hollow men. He describes them as, "…shape without form, shade without color, paralyzed force, gesture without motion…" It is under such circumstances that many individuals just simply withdraw and isolate; while others, at least 1 out of every 175-200, sadly choose to end their own lives.

It is ironic that most depressed persons seek assistance from the family physician, who himself feels least prepared to diagnose such problems or provide effective treatment. In 1970, a study of the members of the Minnesota Academy of Family Physicians ranked depression as one of the most common problems seen in the office. A more recent study by Dr. Jack Frome, Director of Family Medicine Program at the University of Rochester School of Medicine, found that depression ranked 12th among 6000 diagnoses used by family physicians. A study of individual practitioners in Ohio found that emotional disorders such as depression, ranked among the top 10 most frequent problems presented to them in their offices by their patients. While people do not die from depression, it is a disorder that is among the most difficult disorders with which to live. Yet, general practitioners in medicine feel the lack of training to deal with emotional disorders, such as depression. It is one of the most urgent needs for training in medical education and health care service delivery.

In recognition of the serious problems related to the diagnosis and treatment of depression and similar behavioral disorders, consumers have recently been granted, by legislative action, freedom of choice in selecting a health care provider who is trained, experienced, and prepared to identify and constructively respond to patients with these symptoms. Such health care providers generally include clinical psychologists, psychiatrists, clinical social workers, and in some case, marriage and family counselors. These professionals often provide treatment in coordination with the patient's personal physician, the family, the minister, and any other agent of change in the community that the patient depends upon and considers helpful.

It should be noted that there is an increasing emphasis within medical school training to strengthen the course offerings in the area of emotional and behavioral disorders. Physicians are becoming increasingly aware of these disorders and other related behavioral problems. How depression contributes to the onset and exacerbation of physical problems and how it interferes with the treatment and rehabilitation process is now under serious study. Currently, physicians are being trained and urged to make appropriate referrals to the behavioral health care providers within the community who can effectively and efficiently respond and treat the depressed person and his/her family.

Depression Can Be a Normal Response Pattern

Depression is a result of our way of responding to a set of chronic unpleasant and stressful circumstances in our daily life over which we do not have control. This is a state of helplessness. There are times when depression would be considered a normal and typical response for most people undergoing a particular circumstance, such as the death of a loved one. While mild and brief situational depression can be a normal response to a loss or trauma, it is an early warning signal that a more chronic, debilitating level of depression might be on the horizon if appropriate therapeutic counteraction is not taken.

On the other hand, mild chronic depression (dysthymia) can become abnormal over time when any of the following factors are present:

1. A prolonged length of sadness or grief following an event that would ordinarily be associated with a brief period of disappointment or unhappiness.

2. An intense response to a traumatic event so that it becomes an overwhelming emotional state and disrupts a wide spectrum of daily living patterns.

3. The absence of a clear identifying cause or event that produced a state of depression and withdrawal behavior pattern.

4. A lack of any fluctuation in the depressed mood when there are clear changes occurring in the environment and in the social relationships of the individual that would ordinarily be associated with improved emotional arousal and healthy socially oriented behavior.

The Signs and Symptom Patterns of Depression

When the signs and symptoms of depression affect the entire spectrum of a person's life, there is a dire need for a concerted therapeutic program under professional guidance. First, however, we need to study the five components of depression which indicate that the depression is chronic, severe, and in need of professional assessment and treatment.

1. Emotional Ups and Downs

Chronic depression is associated with various strong and unpleasant emotions such as sadness, fear, guilt, shame, and anxiety. The general trend is that of dysphoria, an unpleasant emotional arousal. Psychologists refer to this as "flat affect." It is associated with the lack of facial expression, animation of bodily responses, or any significant arousal to normal environmental-social stimulation. A general feeling of malaise prevails.

2. Motivational Stops and Starts

Dysphoria, an unpleasant emotional state, is associated with passivity, inertia, and a lack of interest in anything. Depressed persons find it most difficult to become active and thereby do not initiate a course of action that might help resolve the depression itself. Hence, depression tends to become chronic and more intense. This passivity generally annoys others and causes them to push the depressed patient into activities, even against their own wishes. Conflict often results with well-intended support persons. Depressed people tend to feel that things are too hard, there is too little time, there is too little energy, and too little incentive to take any action at all. There is a general state of being tired and fatigued. Chronic, pervasive fatigue is one of the most telling signs of depression.

3. *Thinking On and Off*

Chronic depression is also associated with disordered thought pattern and difficulty in processing information. For example, depressed patients often have the inability to "turn off their mind." Hence, they commonly find certain thoughts or images recurring as a rumination. These intrusive thoughts often contribute to sleeping difficulties, concentration problems, and engender various ritualistic behavior patterns. Indecisiveness is another disorder of thinking. In such instances, the patient is unable to sort out the facts of a situation, draw a conclusion, and take decisive action.

Obsessive thinking in the absence of any action is common. There is also the feeling of being overwhelmed with ideas, plans, expectations, and day-to-day events which need to be handled. Being overwhelmed often results in procrastination, indecision, excessive worry, confusion, and frustration. Withdrawal from events and people may be their way to reduce the stress of being overwhelmed. Thought disorder is also seen in the form of self-criticism and self-deprecation talk. This negative self-talk style aggravates depression and results in various self-defeating behaviors. Negative self-talk obstructs action, decreases hope, and interferes with any potential for problem solving or depression relief.

Another way to understand the disorders of thinking in depressed patients is to consider the differences between "depressive" and "healthy" thinking for understanding and organizing one's world of events. Generally speaking, depressed persons tend to organize their experiences in relatively unhealthy and primitive ways. They often make broad, global judgments regarding events, they become overwhelmed with their interpretation of events, and they are likely to interpret events in extreme, negative, absolute, judgmental, and categorical ways. Those with immature or depressive thinking patterns choose the complex, variable, and the diverse aspects of human experience and behavior and reduce them into a few crude and general categories.

In contrast, healthy, mature or non-depressive thinking is characterized by the integration of life events into many different dimensions or categories rather than general qualitative interpretations of events. This distinction between depression and non-depressive thinking is derived from the work of Piaget (1960) when he described the thinking patterns of children. This distinction in thinking patterns is described below:

STYLES OF DEPRESSIVE THINKING

Depressed individuals tend to view their world and experiences as total deprivation or defeat. (Non-dimensional and irreversible). Also, they characterize themselves as losers (categorical, judgmental) and doomed (irreversible). Obviously, depressive thought patterns are non-adaptive and counter-productive for the handling of daily affairs in a person's life (Beck, et.al. 1979). Options and possibility thinking is absent.

On the other hand, healthy and non-depressed individuals tend to view their world and experiences as moderate and multidimensional. They are also more realistic and reversible or resolvable. They also acknowledge life events as being more variable and changeable. They are not boxed in to any position as are depressive individuals. There is more openness to options and possibilities. Possibility thinking is common.

4. Physiological Strengths and Weaknesses
Sleep is frequently disturbed in depression. It is common to experience trouble falling asleep, then awakening early in the

morning after frequent awakening throughout the night and generally restless sleep. It is possible that this sleep disturbance contributes to the fatigue and emotional dysphoria. Eating habits also change drastically, with some people eating less and others tending to eat more when depressed. There is often a disregard for a balanced diet. Sexual activity also diminishes with long periods of abstinence being a common occurrence. Frequently, depressed persons experience mild to moderate headaches, especially in the morning. Most likely, these are related to the anxiety and increased muscle tension which accompanies the worry and physical stress. Likewise, depression is often associated with a dry mouth and numerous other kinds of physical disturbances, generally of the gastrointestinal tract. The irritable bowel syndrome is one example. This could contribute to the loss of interest in eating and the loss of weight.

5. Behavior Passivity and Assertiveness

In depression, there are numerous behavioral changes which occur, some of which are abrupt and severe. Predominant is the tendency to avoid everything. This includes social events with the family, friends, and any opportunity to become socially involved. Physical activity, including leisure and recreational events, becomes almost nonexistent. Communication patterns may change to that of passivity or agitated aggression towards others. There is often excessive crying. Excessive medication taking and alcohol consumption is also likely to occur. In general, there is a marked change in a wide variety of behaviors. Most notably, there is a change towards passivity, withdrawal, and non-engagement. Increasingly deficient social skills are a major symptom of depression.

In contrast, non-depressed persons are generally socially skilled. They are active, quick to respond, relatively insensitive to aversive people, do not miss a chance to react, interact fairly openly in group situations, and elicit from others high rates of positive reinforcement. They are much more socially skilled. Communicatively, they are assertive and forthright.

Measuring the Severity of Depression

A number of questionnaires, rating scales and psychological tests are used by psychologists when providing clinical services to the depressed patient. On the other hand, there are a number of informal rating scales that are also used by professionals. These can be used by the general public as well as to give an index of a person's depression and its severity. For example, a list of adjectives might be presented for a person to check indicating those which primarily describe his or her feelings at any given time. It is recognized that feelings and experiences change from time-to-time. Getting a measure of such change can be very helpful to assess the depression level of a person at various times. Such ratings represent the mood states of the individual at that "slice of time" in his/her life.

One such rating scale was developed by Zuckerman and Associates, 1964. He found that depressed individuals frequently *espouse* the following sample of mood related adjectives:

Alone	Sad	Rejected	Hopeless
Awful	Sunk	Miserable	Lonely
Gloomy	Unhappy	Destroyed	Suffering
Lost	Terrible	Discouraged	Low

Likewise, depressed individuals generally *do not espouse* the following sample of adjectives as being characteristic of their daily mood experience:

Active	Enthusiastic	Good
Alive	Clean	Interesting
Free	Fine	Safe
Healthy	Fit	Strong

On such a rating scale, a scoring procedure would be the following: A plus one point for each adjective espoused in the first set of adjectives noted above and a plus one point for each adjective *not* espoused in the second list. Thus, by adding up the total points of a person, the score is interpreted as representing the severity of depression. Of course, the higher the score the greater the depression.

Rating scales, such as this one, are not only used to assess the presence of depression, but are often used during treatment or over an extended period of time to trace any changes in the severity of the depression. Of course, one would hope that the score would decrease, indicating a lessening of the depression over time and/or as a result of treatment.

In learning some of the basic components of depression, we come to question the "Why" of depression. What causes it? Oh, if we only knew. Causation is a common issue for all diseases and disorders. It sure keeps the scientists active. But we must go on and do the best we can to live productively and happily.

CHAPTER II

THE CAUSES OF DEPRESSION

Why are so many people experiencing depression and the human suffering that is associated with it? One would think that if there was any way to prevent or avoid depression that people would choose the alternative to prevent it and avoid it at all cost. For example, parents should be keenly aware of the potential for depression and attempt to prevent it by developing effective child rearing practices. Unfortunately, depression is not prevented merely by choice. It results from a wide range of circumstances and behavior patterns. Its causes are multiple.

Let us take a look at some of the causes or sources of depression, keeping in mind that any one might be sufficient to cause depression. A combination of factors generally increases the likelihood that depression will occur sometime in the future. There are several causes that can be the trigger for depression and cause its occurrence.

Inadequate Reinforcements or Rewards

Depression is likely to occur whenever there has been a significant reduction in the frequency of reinforcement or reward being experienced daily or a change in the quality of the reward that has been used in the past. This reduction may have been gradual or sudden. Generally speaking, the more or significant the loss, the more devastating it is.

It should be remembered that reinforcement consists of those activities, special privileges, objects and statements we receive from someone as a result of our engaging in appropriate, and desirable behavior. They are primarily provided by those with whom we associate on a daily basis. The major source of social reinforcement is the family, employer, or teacher.

Depressed people generally received inadequate reinforcement during their formative years. It is also possible that the reinforcements which were once provided on a regular basis, have been withdrawn and are no longer available for some reason. For example, the death of a family member who has been a primary source of reinforcement could result in a significant reduction in the reinforcement. Likewise, the reduction of reinforcement could occur as a result of a family member or friend becoming preoccupied with other problems in their life or a shift in social relationships, work associates, or other events. It may be impossible to maintain the same level of reinforcement that has been the case. Also, reinforcement frequency could decrease as a result of a move to a new location or the moving away of a person who has been a primary source of reinforcement. Even though it is explainable and understandable, the reduction in the frequency of reinforcement or the change in the quality of the reinforcement being provided can still result in depression. It is not enough to understand why the frequency or quality of reinforcement has decreased or stopped, but rather, it is necessary to immediately seek new and alternative sources of reinforcement. The more that the reduction in reinforcement can be anticipated and new sources of reinforcement developed, the more likely depression will be prevented or better managed.

Depression can be also inadvertently strengthened by others as they interact with the depressed person. For example, if a depressed person withdraws and remains isolated for a period of time, the family might express more attention and caring. While thinking that they are encouraging to the patient, in fact they might be reinforcing and strengthening the state of depression by their attention and concern. Thus, more withdrawal is likely to occur by the person, in an attempt to elicit and receive more caring behavior from others. Likewise, it is possible that the family will take over responsibilities within the house, or fellow employees will take on various work responsibilities of the depressed person, in an attempt to assist during this time of depression. By so doing, they may be inadvertently reinforcing a depressive behavior pattern.

Insufficient Desirable Behavior to be Reinforced

In the same way that there can be a reduction in frequency and quality of reinforcement in a person's life, so can there be a reduction in desirable behavior patterns which can be reinforced by others.

For example, depressed persons often withdraw and avoid social situations and, as a result, become more unavailable to reinforce due to this social absence and withdrawal. Secondly, depressed persons frequently engage in activities which are not particularly appreciated by others. and thus prompt others to act in a manner which could be perceived as punishing and rejecting. This only leads to further depression. For example, withdrawal might help the depressed person feel less pressure, but it elicits anger, scolding, and criticism from others. Thirdly, depressed persons often act in a depressed pattern, such as not smiling, walking listlessly, or offering little physical expression when talking. This may lead others to counteract by attempting to take charge of the depressed person's life and treating them in a childish manner. This leads to further self-depreciation and depression. Hence, it appears that depression results from a loss of reinforcement and the reduction of those behavior patterns which would ordinarily lead to reinforcement. When people respond with criticism, cajoling, scolding, complaining, and general harassment, the feelings of unworthiness and depression are confirmed.

Chronic Exposure to Aversive Events

Anytime a person is being bombarded or overwhelmed with continuous aversive or noxious events over which he/she has little control, a chronic state of depression may develop. For example, chronic anxiety, pain, or physical disability can contribute to depression because of the continued source of associated unhappiness, stress, frustration, and helplessness. The more one is inhibited from engaging in various enjoyable activities the more depression is likely.

Further examples of aversive events would be chronic criticism from others. Chronic sarcasm, punishment, or threats would be other possible sources of depression. These are all depressing if they are prolonged and severe. They are particularly depressing when there is no counteracting influence such as praise, commendation, achievement, or other forms of positive recognition.

Perhaps a common, but unpleasant example, would be that of an obese spouse. If the obesity is seen as unpleasant and serves as a basis of much criticism and ridicule from the family and others, eventually this person will become depressed. Chronic, unabated criticism, sarcasm, and harassment are powerful aversive comments. Further, if this is associated with social embarrassment, depression worsens. Another example is the young child in the family who is troublesome and difficult to handle. Should the parents choose a course of criticism, negative feedback and overcorrection, this child is likely to become unhappy and depressed. Should this lead to further inappropriate behavior, and the parents increase their criticism and become physically punishing, the depression would likely increase in severity and may even lead to self-harm.

Both of the above situations would likely be associated with the loss of a positive self image and the development of a self-concept which is derogatory, depreciating, and self defeating. Further, the individual may come to expect negative consequences and feedback from others and come to feel doomed to this type of feedback for life. The more the depression, the more the withdrawal and isolation. This leads to more depression. The vicious cycle can be most discouraging.

The State of Helplessness
Depression results from a belief in one's own helplessness (Seligman, 1975). This idea is similar to having a lack of hope of receiving future rewards in life. It is a learned belief based on a history of unsuccessful performance, that one's behavior will not

be effective in attaining any desired goal. There is no expectancy of success. It is not uncommon for people who become depressed to selectively forget about or devalue any success that they have had and, therefore, have little hope or expectancy that success will come their way in the future.

It is important to note that the perception of oneself as a controlling individual is a fundamental factor in self esteem. Anytime we come to accept the loss of control, we develop a feeling of helplessness. Hence, loss of control, or the loss of making things happen, is a basis of helplessness and depression. For example, it is not uncommon for a person who has been recently promoted to a very high position in a company to be depressed. This might seem contradictory, but persons who are in the executive position of a company often delegate the responsibilities to everyone else, and they come to feel or perceive themselves as being less in control over their immediate situation or environment. Other people make things happen, they don't. This also explains why a very beautiful woman might become depressed. For her, compliments or rewards might be based on the fact that she looks beautiful, rather than because of her own performance, accomplishments, or courses of action or effort.

It is likely that helplessness is a state of being in which the person sees no alternative behaviors to use to solve a problem or to get out of a bad situation. It is at this point that a person tends to crumble or break down and become totally unresponsive and passive to others. Therefore, depression is due to the lack of control over the onset of trauma, not trauma itself. One of the best ways to counter depression is to undertake a task and watch the results unfold.

The Six Prominent Features of Learned Helplessness:

- A pattern of passivity, withdrawal, and inadequacy.
- A depletion of Norepinephrine (chemical imbalance).
- A gradual dissipation of personal strength and hope over time.
- A notable lack of assertiveness and forthrightness.
- A belief that there is no way to change or improve things.
- A loss of interest in eating, social, and sexual activity.

In summary, depression can be the result of a long history of increasing helplessness and believing in one's loss of effectiveness. To change the depression depends on becoming more effective. The goal is to achieve mastery in as many different areas of daily living as possible. The successful completion of tasks by a depressed person usually increases optimism, level of aspiration, and the chance of improved performance in subsequent tasks undertaken. This is the primary way to diminish the feelings of helplessness over a period of time.

CHAPTER III

THE TREATMENT OF DEPRESSION

There are generally two types of treatment. One is what we do ourselves to change our plight and state of depression, and the other is treatment we receive from professional resources we consult for help. The combination of these two sources of change, to help us emerge from depression, is the focus of this chapter. Yes, we can do much to help ourselves, and we can learn from the professional therapists to effectively deal with the more difficult issues in our life, present and past, that keep us depressed. Essentially, depression comes about from many sources and reasons, and it can be addressed from many different methods to bring about change. The ultimate desire is to emerge out of depression using all the resources at our disposal.

A. Self Directed Treatment Options

Self-defeating behavioral patterns can be changed over time once a person commits to an intentional decision and plan to alter his/her behavior and live more rationally and less emotionally. It takes time and effort. It takes the support of others and the guidance of many friends. To take on a plan to change your behavior and feelings, select a few actions listed below to which you can commit and follow until the depression is overcome.

1. Learn How to Give and Take Rewards and Reinforcements
It is imperative that depressed people learn to mediate the exchange of reinforcement with each person in their life through the normal course of social interaction. In other words, it is important to learn how to encourage reinforcing statements, activities, events and objects from others. Likewise, it is important

for the depressed person to provide reinforcement to others during social interaction. For example, we all need to learn how to give and receive feedback in the form of a touch, a hug, a statement of reassurance, or an affectionate response. It is also possible to set up a behavioral exchange which results in reinforcement. For example, it might be agreed that the wife help the husband with yard work for two hours if the husband agrees to help her with the housework for two hours. Any behavior exchange, as long as it is reasonably fair and desired, can be entered into by two parties.

In other words, getting too little reinforcement from others can be rectified by learning how to encourage reinforcement from others and how to provide reinforcement to others. This is sometimes referred to as "tit for tat." You do something for me, and I will do something for you. If this sounds somewhat arbitrary and unnatural, let me remind you that this is essentially how all of us behave in our human relationships. We are all involved in activities in which we "repay" special privileges, invitations, assistance, and other actions towards those around us who have done good deeds for us, not necessarily because we need to, but because we want to do it..

Unfortunately, the depressed person generally takes the passive position and waits for others to provide reinforcement, rather than to initiate it themselves. This passivity leaves them vulnerable and very likely to be bypassed and neglected in receiving sufficient reinforcement. This is the basis for a primary depression.

Hence, rewards come in many forms and from many different sources. When these sources diminish or the frequency of these rewards diminish, it is the responsibility of the patient to seek out and develop other activities and varieties of reinforcement.. The family and friends can also do much to assure ongoing frequency and adequacy of rewards at a level which is necessary to live effectively.

2. Learn How to Get Positive Reinforcements for Desirable Behavior

As stated above, it is certainly possible that a depressed individual will behave in depressing ways and others will inadvertently reinforce that depressed behavior by an action which they think will be caring, supportive, and helpful. Unfortunately, this can lead to further and more chronic depression. It is essential that all who are interacting with the depressed person reorder the reinforcements they are providing and make them directly contingent upon appropriate and non-depressive behavior.

A depressive behavior pattern occurs when a person is reinforced for undesirable behavior and is not reinforced for appropriate behavior. On the other hand, non-depressive behavior patterns occur when a person is reinforced for desirable behavior and not reinforced for undesirable behavior. Non-depressive and appropriate behavior is always defined as socially active, emotionally responsive, and self-enhancing. These are good examples of non-depressive behavior patterns. Depressive behavior is the opposite with withdrawal, isolation, and unresponsive patterns. By reordering the reinforcement system which is operating in the life of the depressed person, the family and others can help the depressed person break the vicious cycle of chronic depression.

Therefore, it is necessary for a depressed person to ask or instruct their family and friends to be sure to reinforce only the desirable and appropriate behaviors in the future. They should not be allowed to reward or reinforce undesirable behavior in any way.

3. *Learn How to Receive and Accept Positive Reinforcement from Others*

Depression is generally associated with persons who have not learned to graciously and politely receive positive reinforcing remarks and actions from others. When this is the case, others tend to withhold reinforcing comments and actions, or provide them sparingly, as they do not want to embarrass or create an unpleasant experience for others. Therefore, the frequency of reinforcement can be significantly decreased by virtue of this difficulty in accepting or receiving complimentary reinforcing remarks.

Learn to receive complimentary remarks and events from others by writing 5-8 replies on paper that could be made when being reinforced by a compliment.. Practice these daily by yourself and then try them out with family and friends. They will soon sound more natural and come easily. For example, when somebody compliments you, learn to say, "Thank you," "That was nice of you," or "I appreciate hearing that." On the other hand, upon receiving a gift or a special invitation, it is important that a person who is depressed learn to say, "That was very thoughtful, and I appreciate it," "That was kind of you," or "You are very thoughtful, and I would love to go with you." Success comes with the practice of social skills.

4. *Learn How to Reinforcement Yourself When You Did Well*
It is not only important for our appropriate behavioral actions to be followed by reinforcing statements and actions from others, but we must also learn to be our own source of reinforcement. Patting oneself on the back, at the appropriate times, is a necessary skill in the prevention of depression and in the rehabilitation of the depressed person. To learn this, it is recommended that you write down five or six different activities that were engaged in during the day which deserve positive reinforcement. After each activity noted on the paper, write a statement of compliment, approval, or praise. Remember, it is appropriate and desirable to provide self reinforcement. All of us talk to ourselves, but most of us have learned to do so in non-depressing terms. Depressed people tend to talk to themselves just as much as non-depressed people, but they talk to themselves in more derogatory, self-critical, and self depreciating phrases. Force yourself to change this pattern and speak to yourself, about yourself, in terms which are complimentary, rewarding, and enriching.

5. *Learn How to Use and When to Apply Grandma's Rule*
It was Grandma who taught all of us to first do what she said, and then we could go out and play or eat our dessert. Remember? Therefore, to build reinforcement in your life, first require yourself to make a positive, reinforcing self-reference remark prior to engaging in a highly enjoyable activity.

To make Grandma's Rule work, make use of the chart below. Write down a series of positive reinforcing comments that can be made about yourself and then list a series of activities in which you engage frequently. Then, commit yourself to making one of these positive self-reference statements prior to engaging in one of these high frequency activities. The purpose of this relationship is to increase the likelihood of positive self-reference statements being made in the future. Through psychological research, we have come to learn that those activities in which we engage frequently are often considered to be reinforcing. These can be used to strengthen activities in which we engage less frequently, but would like to do more often.

INCREASING POSITIVE THOUGHTS ABOUT YOURSELF BY APPLYING GRANDMA'S RULE

1. List 5-10 positive self reference statements that you would like to express more often.

2. List 5-10 activities that you now do frequently.

Now, prior to each time you engage in one of these high frequency activities, you are to *first* express any one of the positive self reference statements. Say it aloud or silently; say it to another person or to yourself. Match in sequence any positive thought with any activity noted below.

POSITIVE SELF REFERENCE STATEMENTS	HIGH FREQUENCY ACTIVITIES
1. (I am a great cook.)	1. (Watching TV)
2. (My teeth are attractive.)	2. (Use of cell phone)
3.	3.
4.	4.
5.	5.

6. *Learn How to Write in a Daily Journal*

Using a daily journal to record your daily activities, emotional experiences and social relationships is a very helpful course of action for your health and well-being. Considerable research has shown that journaling has a positive affect on one's health, work productivity, creativity, moods, educational progress, and social-intimate relationships. Journaling is a daily activity for some. For others it is periodic. Whatever frequency you determine, journaling is an activity to be encouraged and promoted.

Buy a journal to use or use an old notebook or writing pad. What is important is that you write and improve your self-expression about your feelings, thoughts, plans, desires, and past experiences. Record positive experiences and feelings as you experience them. Perspective is gained. Enlightenment is realized. Understanding is gleamed. The past is put into an orderly sequence. Emotional healing results as we commit to the process of regular journaling. It is another way to emerge out of depression.

7. *Learn How to Use Your Imagination to Positively Reinforce Yourself*
If one has the ability to imagine or visualize, the technique of covert positive reinforcement can be a very helpful method to change depressed moods. Sit in a comfortable chair or lie on a bed in a relaxed posture. Once relaxed, visualize engaging in an activity which is within the realm of possibility and is likely to occur on a day-to-day basis. For 30-60 seconds, imagine yourself in this particular activity. See yourself as being active and personally involved. Then shift the visualization to that of a scene in which you are being rewarded by someone for doing that activity and for putting forth the necessary effort. This scene is repeated several times. Then imagine a variety of situations in which you are participating in an activity. Always imagine being rewarded for your involvement. Rewards can be in the form of verbal statements, receiving a special privilege or gift, or being allowed to participate in some other activity which is rewarding, relaxing, or highly desirable.

8. *Learn How to Start Some New Activity to Bring Enjoyment into Your Life*
As a result of the loss of behaviors which were the basis of reinforcement, it is imperative that there be encouragement and support for trying new behavior patterns that might lead to new sources of reinforcement. It is common for depressed people who improve in therapy to take up a new hobby or to try an activity that they have wanted to do all their life, but which they have not had

the opportunity to do. They usually find pleasure and reinforcement from these new activities. Likewise, they commonly make new friends and build new associations. Therefore, consider engaging in any activity that might be interesting or intriguing and might open up new friendships.. Family members and friends can urge and support the person in attempting a new activity by going with them or arranging for this activity to be done in an easy and smooth manner. Since there is the problem of overcoming inertia or passivity, it often takes considerable urging, encouragement, and mild pressure from others to attempt a new activity. When this occurs, consider this as positive encouragement and not negative prodding.

9. *Learn How to Increase Your Social Value in the Eyes of Others* Reinforcement is more likely to come when people have high social stimulus value. This includes how one dresses, wears makeup, styles the hair, and uses facial expression. These factors, among others, strongly determine the occurrence of expressed reinforcement from others. Unfortunately, we live in a culture in which the appearance of the individual is important and serves as a basis of our interpersonal response patterns. Therefore, since there is a tendency among depressed people to neglect their appearance and become less attractive, it is essential that others be allowed to assist and help the depressed person increase their social stimulus value. The rule to follow is: dress appropriately for the occasion. Do not purposely dress to be noticed, but to be acceptable for the occasion. Being with a group of known friends is a start, but it should give confidence to proceed to larger social groups.

Hence, depression is partly a direct outgrowth of a deficiency in social skills. To counteract this, it is important to learn ways in which negative and depressing behaviors can be changed and how a person can become more socially effective. For example, assertive behavior, once learned, reduces the need to avoid situations and groups. Once we feel we can control our negative thinking and our irrational ideas and believe that we can deal with a wide variety of interpersonal ideas, then we have a basis of competence and a greater likelihood of remaining involved in the events around us.

10. Learn How to Diversify Your Activities and Interests
To counteract the state of learned helplessness, it is important to engage in a wide variety of activities throughout the week and not become dependent upon one type of activity. It is certainly possible to experience a helplessness pattern in one area of life, while not experiencing helplessness in another area. To the degree in which diversification is present, depression is prevent or minimized. Friends and family should do everything possible to help the depressed person seek opportunities which will lead to effectiveness, mastery, success, and achievement in several areas of life. Thus, the achievement level in one area will counteract the sense of helplessness in other areas of life. This calls for creativity and taking a risk to try out a new activity or venture.

11. Learn How to Visualize Doing Things Better and More Successfully
If a depressed person is capable of visualizing and imagining clearly, the method of covert visual rehearsal can be used effectively. In this situation, one is asked to assume a relaxed posture and close the eyes. The individual then imagines a situation which has been depressing and has been associated with feelings of helplessness. In the visualization, then imagine handling the same situation in an effective, positive, and forthright manner, but in a gradual, graded sequence. In other words, the situation is conquered, resolved or handled successfully in the visualization. Once clearly visualized, shift to a scene in which one is being reinforced for effectiveness and mastery in that situation. As a result of repeating this sequence on numerous occasions and similar scenes for several days in a row, there is an increased chance of being successful in undertaking efforts to resolve problems and confront difficult situations. The result of increased success contributes to a sense of effectiveness rather than helplessness.

12. Learn How to Reduce Your Levels of Physical Tension
There are several ways to reduce your level of tension and associated feelings of anxiety. Two of the most frequently used

methods involve a sequence of deep breathing and muscle relaxation.

Deep breathing is the process of inhaling deeply and holding your breath for 3-5 seconds and then slowly exhaling to the count of five. Inhale ….. Hold ….. Exhale. Again, Inhale ….. Hold ….. Exhale. Repeat this 5-7 times and do it 3-5 times daily. Never force it or do it quickly or rapidly. That will result in a state of hyperventilation. Go slowly and systematically for best results to achieve relaxation. The process changes the balance of Oxygen and Carbon Dioxide in the blood stream and ultimately the brain.

Muscle relaxation is the process of training your muscles to let go and relax. Muscles are like rubber bands. You can stretch them which are like a state of tension or you can let them go and they will return to a state of relaxation or calmness. Several times daily, engage in muscle relaxation. Tense and hold for five seconds and then let go. While tense feel the tension and discomfort. When you let go, feel or notice the relief or absence of tension. Start with the feet and legs, go to the mid-body, them proceed to the chest. Feel the increased level of relaxation already achieved. Then proceed to tense and relax the shoulders, arms, neck, and areas of the face. Finally, sit quietly and feel the difference between the state of tension and the state of relaxation. Muscles are not meant for tension, but for relaxation, unless needed to meet life's demands.

*13. Learn How to Make and Use a **TO DO LIST** to Increase your Daily Accomplishments*
Everyone works from a **TO DO LIST** to assure that things get done in a timely manner. It is a way to make our time efficient and not forget what needs to be accomplished each day. When depressed, there is a tendency to overlook such a list or disregard it completely. Hence, a **TO DO LIST** is good to help combat and overcome depression. Such a list can be drawn up daily or weekly. It is best to be drawn up with a support family person. The important thing is to have list that is reasonable and doable. It is also important to assure a positive reinforcement statement or action each time the depressed person engages in an activity on the

list. Here is an example of how a **TO DO LIST** can be arranged and made functional.

<u>MY TO DO LIST</u>

<u>DAILY</u>
1. Meditate and pray for renewed energy and vitality
2. Write an entry in my journal
3.
4.
5.

<u>WEEKLY</u>
1. Take a walk
2. Attend some type of social event, i.e., go to a movie or church meeting
3.
4.
5.

<u>PERIODICALLY</u>
1. Write a poem
2. Talk on the phone with an old friend
3.
4.
5.

Rewards or reinforcements for any active accomplished could be anything such as candy, a special event, points for later use and go to an activity of importance, and a preferred food or meal. The important thing is to reward immediately not hours or days later. Have fun rewarding and enjoy the **TO DO LIST** activities.

A chart has been provided (see above) to help you in your process of visualization to rehearse handling difficult situations in daily living. Focus on those tasks which are meaningful to you, personally.

B. **Professionally Directed Treatment Options**

Not all behavior change is brought about by self-directed efforts. Professional guidance and directed strategies are also needed. Professionals can give better clarity and direction to bring about change. Professionals can hold a person accountable better and provide the steps of change more clearly. Some changes require a multi-dimensional approach and may require the consultation of other professionals as well. Personally do what you can do, and then accept professional help to assure success in the plan to come out of the darkness of depression. Here are some of the strategies professionals use to help a depressed person.

1. Thought Stopping is Used to Control Your Depressive Thinking
When a person withdraws and does not engage in activities which could promote reinforcement, they often develop and engage in disorders of thinking such as rumination and obsessive thought patterns. Frequently these thought patterns are self critical and self depreciating. The more that these kinds of thoughts occur, the more a person tends to withdraw, and then it is less likely that reinforcing behaviors will take place. To combat these ruminations and obsessive-negative thought patterns, the technique of *thought stopping* is often found to be helpful. In this procedure, the patient is advised to yell the word "no" or "stop" several times in succession each time a negative thought occurs. This is to be repeated on every occurrence of any negative, self defeating and depressing thought as a way to interfere with it and stop it from reoccurring. This procedure should also be practiced daily by focusing on these thoughts and then yelling. "No, no, no, no, no." Repeat it 20-30 times during the practice session.

In public, the patient is advised to whisper or think the word "no" or "stop" repeatedly when negative thoughts occur. This sequence can be varied by saying both words alternately. These words should be said five or ten times in a row, or at least until the negative, depressing thought pattern terminates. For most people, this procedure needs to be used over a course of several weeks, but eventually the frequency of these depressing and self defeating thoughts diminish and come under control.

2. Correct Irrational Thoughts by Thinking More Rationally and Realistically
Depressed individuals commonly have a long history of irrational thoughts. A few examples of irrational thinking include the following:

a.   That is a dire necessity to be loved or approved by almost everyone for virtually everything he does.

b.   That one should be thoroughly competent, adequate, and achieving in all possible respects.

c.   That certain people are bad, wicked, or villainous and that they should be severely blamed and punished for their sins.

d.   That it is terrible, horrible, and catastrophic when things are not going the way I would like them to go.

e.   That human unhappiness is always externally caused and that people have little or no ability to control their sorrows or rid themselves of their negative feelings.

f.   That if something is or may be dangerous or fearsome, one should be terribly occupied with and upset about it.

g.   That it is easier to avoid facing many life difficulties and self responsibilities than to undertake more rewarding forms of self discipline.

h.   That the past is all-important and that because something once strongly affected one's life, it should indefinitely do so.

These irrational thoughts often become more pervasive and frequent over time. They often are associated with withdrawal and lead the person to engage in associated irrational behavior. To increase one's awareness of irrational thoughts and thinking, the Triple Column Technique is suggested. The Triple Column Technique is shown in the chart below. You are encouraged to write down a series of irrational ideas that are frequently considered throughout the day. Then, identify the times when these irrational ideas occur, note what makes them irrational, and state how they could be altered to be more realistic. For example, one irrational idea that many depressed people exhibit is as follows: "I can't be happy unless I'm loved by everyone."

Such ideas need to be subjected to analysis and correction. To continue them only prevents the depression from abating and coming under control. A professional can help to identify these thoughts and patterns. Often it is easier for a person to share with a therapist than with a family member, and thus, they can dig deeper into their thought patterns with a therapist. To help, a family member might also assist in identifying these kinds of thoughts, analyzing them, and correcting them . This must be done in a supportive way and with much patience and tolerance.

From the above example, it should be noted that one cannot be loved by all and need not be loved by all. One's value and happiness depends on many factors not just love. People could in fact love you, but you may not know it or accept it (Beck, et.al. 1979). This is the process of correcting irrational thinking.

THE TRIPLE COLUMN TECHNIQUE

1. Analyze your thoughts that are associated with depression by filling out the spaces below whenever a depressed feeling occurs.

2. Do this for at least 10 different occasions of depression. Be as specific as possible.

Events Which Triggers Depressed Feelings	Actual Thoughts Associated With Depressed Feelings	Facts To Help Change the Depressed Thoughts to Reality
1. Making a mistake when trying a new recipe.	"I'm always a failure."	The directions were wrong. I made a mistake but I don't always do that. A mistake is not equal to failure.

3. *Assertive Communication Will Help Meet the Needs of the Patient and not Let them be Taken Advantage of by Others*
One of the major behavioral deficits among depressed people is the absence of assertive communication skills. It is difficult for depressed people to ask for assistance, express feelings, opinions and preferences, or to say "no" to someone making an unreasonable request. It is also difficult to invite others to do something, negotiate differences, resolve conflict, or put an end to

harassment. Unfortunately, there is a tendency to withdraw, isolate and avoid these kinds of situations rather than confront them. The answer to depression is partly found in the development of assertive skills as a way to become more socially confident and less fearful of others. A therapist will help you accomplish this.

To learn assertive skills, it might be desirable for the patient to take a class at the local junior college or a seminar offered in the community by a respected professional. There are a number of books on the market which teach assertive skills and are written for the lay person. A listing of several books is noted at the back of this book. It is also possible to learn assertiveness by observing and imitating people who are known for their effective assertiveness. Assertiveness can also be learned through imagery. In this, the person is asked to relax, close the eyes and imagine or visualize being a very assertive person handling interpersonal conflicts in an assertive, effective and socially skilled manner. By visualizing several situations in which assertive behavior is successfully emitted, one is encouraged to employ it in real life. There is likely to be a good degree of carryover to actual situations in daily living from the imaginative scene.

In the chart below, assertive behavior is distinguished from non-assertive behavior and aggressive behavior. By reviewing this chart, it is possible to clearly see that non-assertive behavior contributes to being rejected and being counterpoised by others. If a person cannot resolve conflict, frustration, and defeat, depression results. The middle column in the chart is assertive behavior, the ideal objective to be attained by all of us in our social relationships. By looking over the various aspects of assertive behavior, in contrast to non-assertive and aggressive behavior, the patient can learn from his therapist how to behave in social situations with others. In other words, the objective is to become declarative, forthright, confident, direct, expressive, considerate, honest and respectful.

THE NON-ASSERTIVE, ASSERTIVE, AND AGGRESSIVE BEHAVIOR PATTERNS

Non-Assertive…is failing to stand up for oneself, or standing up for oneself in such an ineffectual manner that one's rights are easily violated.
Assertive… is standing up for oneself in such a way that one does not violate the basic rights of another person. It's a direct honest and appropriate expression of one's feelings and opinions.
Aggressive…is standing up for oneself in such a way that the rights of the other person are violated in the process. It's an attempt to humiliate or put down the other person.

	Non-assertive	Assertive	Aggressive
Characteristics:	Indirect, self-denying, hidden bargains, emotional dishonesty.	Direct, expressive, leveling, Self-enhancing, supportive, firm.	Direct, domineering at expense of others, cutting off communication, put downs
Your feelings when you engage in this behavior:	Hurt, anxious at the time, and possibly angry later.	Confident, self-respect at the time and later.	Righteous, superior, deprecatory of others at the time, and possibly guilty later.
The other person's feelings when you engage in this behavior:	Guilty or superior.	Valued, respected, Confident, May attempt to imitate you.	Hurt, humiliated, Embarrassed,. Devastated
The other person's feelings when you engage in this behavior:	Irritation, pity, disgust.	Respectful.	Angry, vengeful. Hostile.

4.   Criticism Can be Constructive and Beneficial
Criticism, sarcasm, and other forms of put-down statements are potentially devastating to anyone. The person who is mildly depressed and continues to be criticized becomes increasingly depressed and defeated. It should also be remembered that criticism is a form of feedback and we can all learn from it. There are numerous ways in which a therapist can help you deal with criticism so that such remarks can be countered to minimize their effect. To do so, a therapist will follow certain basic principles, as outlined below. Although it is difficult to employ these principles or guidelines when depressed and while experiencing under unfair criticism, they can be powerfully helpful in managing any critical feedback. It is usually helpful to discuss any criticism with supportive family member or friends as well as your therapist.

THE POWER OF CRITICISM

1. *Criticism is usually an exaggerated statement for the purpose of directing your attention to some specific area of your life and behavior patterns. Therefore, do not concern yourself with the entire exaggerated comment, but look for "the nugget of truth" and try to understand the specific point of concern.*

2. *Criticism is often stated in general, non-specific terms, so it may be difficult to know exactly what the point of reference is or what happened to create the need for the criticism. Therefore, it is often helpful to ask for several specific examples which illustrate the expressed criticism. Try to obtain as many specific facts and direct observations as possible.*

3. *Criticism commonly serves to initiate argumentation and debate. Hurt feelings generally develop as a result of the argumentation rather than the criticism itself. Therefore it is generally helpful to identify one aspect of the criticism that you can agree with and thereby minimize any argument from developing.*

4. *Criticism can be constructive and a basis for personal growth.   . Therefore, rather than argue over the facts of a criticism, it is generally beneficial to ask for specific suggestions as to how a particular problem might be improved upon or what specific action can be taken to minimize the situation that led to the criticism.*

5. *Criticism, particularly persistent criticism, can be very destructive if you have no response at all to make to it and merely stand there passively. The Broken Record Technique has been very helpful in such situations. Here, you make a neutral response to the criticism and then continue to repeat that response over and over to the individual who is persistent in being critical. For example, the statement, "I understand what you are saying," might be one such statement that could be repeatedly made, rather than defending yourself or arguing correctness of the critical remark being made.*

6. *Criticism about one particular aspect of your behavior pattern does not imply that you are totally inept or incompetent in other areas of your life. It is important to separate the criticism of one area in your life from other areas which may be beyond any critical comment or evaluation. Then try to profit from the criticism.*

7 .*Criticism is one way in which blame is placed upon others rather than accepting responsibility for one's own behavior. While there may be some truth to a critical comment, it is very important that the situation be thoroughly understood. This helps so that no one accepts fault for an action other than that which is rightly theirs to assume. Most situations cannot be blamed on any one person and calls for the sharing of responsible*

As you can see, criticism can be destructive and demoralizing. On the other hand, criticism can be the basis for making positive changes and moving forward in life. A therapist can help us learn from criticism. Not all parts of a criticism may be true. Some parts may be true. Learn from those aspects of the criticism and downplay the other. As one therapist said, "There is gold in them there hills." Find the gold and bypass the non-gold.

5.   Communication Skills Can Facilitate or Obstruct Social Relationships

Depression generally results when a person does not utilize effective communication skills to foster conversation, solve problems and develop relationships. Although communication skills are complex, there are a few simple techniques and principles that can be utilized in most interpersonal situations. A few statements that *facilitate* communication and relationships are as follows:

a. I want, I feel, I like and I don't like statements
b. Asking a direct question

c. Listing options and choosing among them
d. Bargaining
e. Self-disclosure
f. Expressing mixed feelings
g. Asking for feedback
h. You are good; you did something good complimentary statements

A few statements that *obstruct* communication and relationships are as follows:

a. Overly long statements
b. Statements which say you are bad, you did something bad
c. You should, you ought to statements
d. Sarcasm, commanding putdowns, threats
e. Communication cutoff
f. Unnecessary apologies and self-effacing statements
g. Attacking with a new or different issue
h. Ignoring important messages of others

Chronic depression is also a result of chronic aversive and noxious events in your life. This may be in the form of chronic anxiety, pain, criticism, sarcasm, threat of punishment, or other negative effects. It is the *confrontive* approach which is most helpful in controlling these kinds of aversive events. Once assertive and communication skills are learned and applied, an individual has the skills to cope in an effective and non-combative manner in a variety of unpleasant situations. Therapy is the place to learn these communication skills.

From the above types of communication statements, it is obvious that professional guidance would be helpful, and it will take considerable time in learning to implement them effectively. Should it appear that a lack of communication and assertive skills contribute to the chronic anxiety and depression, I would recommend that a professional develop this skill area with you (Strayhorn, 1979).

6. *Personal Mastery Comes About in Graded and Incremental Steps*

To counter one's feelings of helplessness, one must learn that anyone can master numerous types of situations. A history of mastery inoculates us against the most severe form of depression and develops a sense of self efficacy. Some people force themselves to work excessive hours to see if they can make something happen and make their efforts produce some results. Others might argue, fight or be excessively confrontive to bring some action about in others. Depression is minimized when one's behavior produces change or leads to goal attainment.

It is interesting to note the people who experience mastery in everything they do. This might be because they are very able individuals or because they only take on tasks which they can successfully complete. Hence, they do not learn how to cope with failure, anxiety, frustration, or disappointment. These individuals might be referred to as the "golden young people." Psychological research has vividly shown that people who only have mastery in their younger years have a tendency to fail in coping with stress and may later break down and experience a variety of severe psychological disorders such as depression.

To achieve mastery, a therapist can help you utilize a graded task assignment format. This was originally developed by psychologist Elaine Burgess, formerly of Drake University. At first, engage in a very simple task, such as making a simple telephone call and asking for information. Once completed and done well, try a second level task of increasing difficulty such as taking a gift back and exchanging it for something different. Once this is done effectively and with mastery, take on a more complex task, such as arranging a party. Each time, the task should be more complex but within one's abilities to perform the task and to do so successfully. Thus, the person experiencing success at each task level, builds competence and is encouraged. This gives an opportunity for others to reinforce and commend the person for their accomplishments and provides opportunity for self reinforcement. To start a task and then give up, or to fail, would only worsen depression and enhance the habit of prematurely terminating and withdrawing from tasks and activities.

To help plan a graded task assignment for a patient, a therapist can use the chart below. Follow the planning steps as outlined. Use the plan for several weeks during therapy, at least, and increase the difficulty level gradually from week to week.

MY PERSONAL GRADED MASTERY ASSIGNMENT

1. List 5-10 tasks you *will do* this week.
2. Make an appointment with yourself to do them during the week. Specify when, where, how, with whom, etc.
3. List how you will reward yourself after doing each task. Use the same reward several times or use different rewards.
4. Progress from simple to moderate tasks. Avoid difficult tasks for now. They come later in the process.
5. Work out your personal plan with someone who is supportive and encouraging.

SIMPLE TASKS	REWARD FOR DOING THE TASK
1.	1.
2.	2.
3.	3.
MODERATE TASKS	**REWARD FOR DOING THE TASK**
1.	1.
2.	2.
3.	3.

This exercise demonstrates that therapy is more that just "talk therapy." Cognitive behavioral therapy is talk and a lot learning exercises. It is an active process. It is a process of revamping a person's behavioral patterns and making them more effective and relevant to the goals a person/patient desires to achieve.

CHAPTER IV

THE IMPACT OF DEPRESSION

What to Do Before the Therapist is Consulted

The treatment of depression is complex and must be approached in a systematic and progressive manner. Professional consultation is essential for any person who has been depressed for a period of time. To overcome this debilitating disorder without systematic and professional guidance is rare.

Prior to undertaking a professionally guided course of psychotherapy, the following steps should be considered:

1. Utilize the Balm of Time, but Prepare to Take Action
Depression may be a normal response to a stressful event. There are times when people respond to a situation with depressed mood and behavior. If this is the case, do not feel guilty, but the depression should be time limited and certainly not defeating. However, if the depression lingers beyond several weeks or months, it is probably a state that is beyond what is typical or normal for the situation. Then, professional help must be seriously considered and entered into willingly and with hopeful expectations.

2. Develop a Strong Social Support System
This should consist of the family, relatives, friends, business associates, ministers and any other person who can generate hope and the expectation of change. The more all these people openly communicate together, the better. When soliciting the support of others, a therapist can help you choose those that live an anti-depressing life style and who can be sources of reinforcement and pleasant events. They should be quick to encourage, quick to

strengthen, and quick to praise and commend. They should be tolerant, empathic, and understanding. They should be able to engage you in a range of activities which are anti-depressing and uplifting. On the other hand, they should not be prone to speak in platitudes and trite phrases. They should not be people who try to cheer you up with false smiles or laughter, or who are themselves depressed.

3. Get an Idea of How Depressed you really are Before You Start Treatment
One way is for the therapist to obtain information, chart, and graph several behavioral and emotional aspects of the depressed person's way of life. Once these have been obtained, they can be used as a base-line index of the pretreatment level of depression. These same observations can be repeated later to assess whether there has been any productive change as a result of the therapy program initiated.

For example, it might be good for your therapist to chart the following kinds of information prior to the initiation of any treatment program:
    a. The hours per day spent up and active. This is called "up time."
    b. The number of people per day with whom there has been contact or involvement. Call this "together time."
    c. The Subjective Units of Disturbance at different intervals throughout the day is recorded on a scale of 1 to 100). This will indicate the level of emotional disturbance or depression that is being felt. This is called a SUDS Scale.
    d. The number of times per day that a self-derogatory remark was made. This is called "negative self-talk" or "stinkin' thinkin'."

4. Assess How Depressing Your Social and Physical Environment Really is
It is possible to simply divide one's environment and daily activities into two general categories. On the chart below, with your therapist, conduct an analysis of your environment and daily life events so that you specifically identify people, places and things that you associate with depressing or non-depressing effects on you. Accordingly, then, one should be careful to seek out those

people, places and things which are non-depressing on a day-to-day basis and avoid those people, places, and things which are depressing.

In this manner, a person's mood and general motivational level can be influenced and altered by selectively spending time and devoting energy to those events and people which are definitely anti-depressing. Thus, by surrounding yourself with anti-depressing circumstances, your own mood can be elevated and your spirit encouraged. With your therapist, complete the chart below to better assess the influence of depressing and anti-depressing events on you.

Successful Therapy

In undertaking a treatment program for depression, it is helpful to know what defines success. Consider these guidelines:

1. Successful treatment occurs when a patient believes that his/her behavior again produces gratification and that he/she comes to see himself as an effective human being. That is, there should be an obvious relationship between the person's behavior and positive, pleasant, and supportive feelings.

2. Successful treatment occurs when the patient learns how to gain access to a wide variety of sources of positive reinforcement or rewards. We need to learn the skills of how to solicit reinforcement from others and how to provide it to oneself. This skill leads to a degree of optimism and hope.

3. Successful treatment occurs when the lessons learned in therapy serve a preventative role in the future life of the patient. It is necessary to resolve past problems and the present level of depression. To prevent future depressions from occurring one must acquire the skills of problem solving, assertiveness, and decision making.

4. Successful treatment occurs when a patient acquires a wide repertoire of coping and mastery skills to minimize the impact of noxious or aversive events which will occur in the future. These include but are not limited to relaxation, assertiveness, open communication and pleasure seeking behavior.

5. Successful treatment occurs when a patient can demonstrate on graphs and charts that his/her daily behavior is more socially involved, less self-depreciating and more initiating of new social contacts and activities. In other words, if the charts and graphs show a change, the depression is probably changing. Charting is merely one

way to reveal actual behavior change, and thus, be
encouraged.

The treatment of depression generally consists of 15 to 25 sessions
at regular intervals. It is not uncommon for therapists to prefer that
patients come weekly for the first several weeks of therapy, then
curtail the frequency to that of twice monthly sessions for the next
10 to 12 weeks, and then gradually reduce the frequency to every
other month for several months. Once treatment progress has been
achieved and there is evidence of stability, termination is
considered. Most therapists prefer to see a patient in 3 or 4 months
for several booster sessions thereafter. These follow-up sessions
might be scheduled at regular intervals over the next year or
scheduled, as needed.

Most therapists, particularly those that practice cognitive behavior
therapy, make use of systematic homework assignments to assist in
bridging the gap between the therapy sessions and the real life
environment. For example, homework assignments might be given
in socialization, such as going to a specific social event or going
shopping in a particular store. On the other hand, homework
assignments might include assertive communication or practicing a
particular technique such as thought stopping. Also, friends and
families are often instructed to assist in certain ways so they are
able to aid in the utilization of the treatment techniques being
learned in therapy.

Success in the work place depends on everyone's contribution. No
one can afford to ignore the early signs of depression. It affects
approximately 10-20% of the population. The good news is that, in
more than 80% of cases, treatment is effective. The combination
of psychotherapy and appropriate antidepressant medication has
been demonstrated to be the most effective treatment plan to help a
depressed person return to a satisfactory functioning life at home
and in the work place. It is not a matter of coping with depression,
but changing it by changing lifestyle, circumstances, and
behavioral patterns, as outlined above.

An Ounce of Prevention

Although our focus has been on the treatment of depression, it would be wise to now direct our attention to the principles of child rearing that are critical to the prevention of depression. It should be observed that there is no absolute formula to totally prevent depression. However, there are general guidelines that can be helpful to parents in the raising of children. When applied systematically, the probability that depression will become a problem is reduced. There are four basic principles that can be effectively implemented in developing the parent-child relationship that guard against depression.

The four principles are as follows:
 1. Provide a variety of positive reinforcements or rewards on a daily basis to a child but only for appropriate behavior.

2. Provide a wide range of opportunities for the child to learn various skills which will enable them to earn positive reinforcement (e.g. praise, recognition) throughout their childhood and adult years.

3. Identify and minimize or eliminate any events which create aversive, unpleasant or noxious experiences for the child over an extended period of time.

4. Teach and demonstrate that helplessness is not an option and that effective action can always be attempted in dealing with any situation, no matter how difficult it appears to be.

These general principles can be implemented by any parent. Granted, a program of implementation would require considerable planning and parental cooperation to make it workable as part of family life. The following parenting skills are based on the above principles and have an anti-depressing influence on a child if employed conscientiously by the parent. Family therapy and individual therapy can be very helpful to assure the four principles of prevention noted above are understood and implemented.

Parenting Skills to Prevent Depression in Children

1. *Build a positive self concept.* It is important that parents praise and commend a child for any effort towards accomplishment of a task or skill activity. It is through honest approval and affirmation that a child comes to be self accepting as a worthy and competent individual. It is also essential that parents teach the child to be self rewarding for all accomplishments. For example, when a child completes a project, as a result of much effort and hard work, the parent might say, "That is excellent, I am very proud of you." Further, the parent might go on to say, "…and you can be proud of yourself" or, "You can be pleased with yourself for that work. I hope you feel happy with what you have just accomplished." Encourage a child to state a self enhancing comment for work well done and positive effort put forth. Express these statements frequently, but be honest and sincere at all times.

2. *Reduce any perfectionism demands.* Perfectionism may be a child's attempt to avoid criticism, scolding, and disapproval. Likewise, it may be an attempt to solicit approval and acceptance from others, especially from the parents. Unfortunately, perfectionism is essentially impossible, so it carries with it inevitable defeat, failure, and frustration. The parents must be careful to set their expectations and standards at a reasonable level, commensurate with their child's age, ability, previous experiences and personal preferences. Also, provide them with liberal acceptance and positive reinforcement which is not based on perfectionism. Enjoyment and satisfaction may be more important to emphasize to prevent depression.

3. *Develop a listening ear.* Throughout our life, but especially in childhood, we want people around us who have the skill of listening and who have time to listen. Too often parents are anxious about how their children act and then respond to this anxiety by lecturing, demanding, and generally talking *at* their children rather than with them. If parents don't listen attentively, their children will find others who will listen. On the other hand,

the children might just stop talking, withdraw, avoid and generally become less than socialized. This withdrawal and passive behavior is the child's pathway to depression. By listening, your child might learn to listen as well.

4. *Develop close family relationships.* Family life sets the occasion for positive experiences to be enjoyed with those who are important to us. The family home is the stage for learning behavioral skills, developing interpersonal relationships, and learning to bond together. The broader the family life activities the better. By engaging in a variety of positive events together, a sense of belonging to a unit and a support system is developed. Weekly family life activities and learning experiences cannot be overemphasized. Community resources, such as the church, can be invaluable in building family strength.

5. *Develop problem solving and decision making skills.* Family life is the arena for the development of basic problem solving and decision making skills. The more that these skills are acquired, the more the child will utilize these skills in his/her own social interactions among peers. Children learn these essential skills as a result of daily living experiences and by observing the parents make decisions and solve problems.

Below is a problem solving flow chart to illustrate a sequential way to teach problem solving to children. Follow this system as practical everyday problems occur in family living.

THE PROBLEM SOLVING PROCESS

1. Identify the problem
   a. Isolate the situation
   b. Be as specific as possible
2. Generate all possible options
   a. Do not judge any option
   b. Wild ideas are welcome
   c. Produce as many options as possible
   d. Combining options is acceptable
3. Eliminate any obviously poor choices
4. Examine the remaining options, one at a time.
   a. List all possible negative consequences of this option
   b. List all possible positive consequences of this option
   c. Eliminate an option if it is generally negative
   d. Go on to next option (steps a-c)
   e. Compare all remaining options
   f. Select most positive option
5. Generate all possible ways to implement the selected option
6. Implement the selected strategy to solve the identified problem

6. Develop assertive communication skills. Being able to communicate in a forthright assertive manner is of utmost importance in the development of behavior patterns that prevent depression in later life. Happy is the person who can express his/her own preferences, request assistance from others when needed, say "no" when there is a desire not to participate, and can express appreciation, gratitude, joy, disappointment, sorrow, sadness, anger, and other feelings or opinions. The more a person can relate in a forthright and honest manner, the more effective he/she will feel. Changing a person's communication and problem solving skills from being passive to being assertive is critical in the prevention of depression. Likewise, changing a person's communication pattern from being aggressive to being assertive is just as important to prevent depression, as aggressive behavior may cause excessive guilt and further social withdrawal. Aggression may also cause further rejection.

7. *Prevent the loss of a parent during the child's formative years.* Research studies seem to indicate that adult depression is significantly more likely to occur if there has been a loss of a parent in the child's life prior to age 17. Although the loss of a parent by death seems to be the most potentially depressing event in the life of a young child or early adolescent, the loss by means of divorce may have a very similar effect. This can be particularly true if the divorcing parent ignores, rejects, or has as prolonged time of noninvolvement with the young child. Perhaps our laws of joint custody will help prevent this parental loss for children. It has been said that the best gift a father can give his children is to love their mother. Obviously, a strong marriage and a deeply committed loving relationship between husband and wife can be one of the most potent factors in preventing the occurrence of depression during childhood, adolescence, or later in life. Loss can also be the prolonged absence of a parent due to business trips. Likewise loss can be a result of long work hours of both parents.

Hence, the prevention of depression cannot be guaranteed, but we can develop skills and participate in specific activities that increase the probability of preventing depression. As these kinds of skills and experiences are acquired in early childhood, the more likely depression will be prevented in later life. Certainly, the life experiences of childhood and early adolescence are critical to the prevention or development of depression. Skills such as assertiveness, must be constantly sharpened and improved as we enter the adult years, so that we become more effective and develop mastery in a wide variety of areas in daily living. Life without areas of mastery or competency may produce vulnerability to depression.

8. *Help the child learn that others do think well of them.* It is vitally important that a child get an accurate understanding of what others think of them. Children often misperceive the view of others

and think in a more paranoid manner than what is true. Help the child know that he/she is loved, appreciated, and valued by others. Be specific. Help restructure wrong perceptions and understandings by a child. Be very clear on this with children. Monitor it closely.

The Empty Nest or the Empty Woman

In women, there is a higher probability that depression will occur later in life. The term "the empty nest syndrome" has often been used to describe the depressed woman who has a sense of loss when children mature and leave the home. Perhaps it would be more humane to accept the term "post-mothering conflict," as it has been utilized in Rational Emotive Therapy (Oliver, 1977).

As has been stated above, there is a direct relationship between depression and the occurrence of prior stressful events in a person's life. Much research tends to confirm the observations that depressed persons experience more environmental stress prior to the onset of depression than other medical and mental health patients. Certainly the separation of children from the home could qualify as a significantly stressful event in the life of the mother. This is true if she is home full time or part time, or works full time or part time. The stress is best understood when we consider that women have come to base their self-esteem and self-worth on their mothering relationships within the home. Mothering has become the central portion of a woman's life and central to her perception of herself as a person. This mothering relationship is emphasized over her other areas of competency, interests, accomplishments or adult relationships.

It is interesting to reflect on the demand that society places upon women in terms of child rearing. She is held responsible for the rearing of a physically healthy, psychologically sound, educationally accomplished, socially adept, and self-fulfilled child. The child is expected to leave the home in early adulthood with a smooth transition and without trauma to anyone. Her children are expected to live happily ever after.

When the children leave the home she is forced into involuntary "retirement," often unprepared and unwilling to accept the fact that retirement has now become a reality. She retires from the only serious work she has ever known and from an endeavor in which she has developed extraordinary skills. In the home she exercised power commensurate with the responsibilities bestowed upon her. She retires from an arena in which she has had the power to influence, the power to control the lives of others, and the power to implement decisions she made. Although she may not even receive a gold medal for her services, she is expected to take heart in the future successes of her children and enjoy the reminiscence of successful motherhood.

Once bereft of this power, with or without alternative sources of self-esteem and self-worth, she faces a life and a home which is now empty. It is a loss of persons, but more importantly, a loss of control, of power, of reinforcement, and of influence. This is especially true of mothers who have been over-committed, over-protective and over-involved in the lives of her children. She now faces a time in her life where she lives in an empty nest, and faces life as an empty woman. It is the empty woman who is depressed. She feels the loss of hope, power, and reinforcement and now feels helpless.

Certainly at this time, if not before, she must shift her focus of attention and energy to develop a new self concept, new skills and to launch new activities. She cannot live happily in the shadows of her children's ongoing lifestyle, merely reminisce over past memories, or obsess about how things ought to be. This is the time to seriously reframe and redefine her purposes, goals and hopes for her future. This is often done through her employment and her volunteer involvements in the community.

Correct Irrational Thinking

All parents need to identify and alter any irrational thoughts or false hopes that might have regarding themselves and others. For example, a parent might have one of the following irrational thoughts:

1. "I have failed as a mother; therefore, I am no good."

2. "I should have done things differently."

3. "If they really cared for me, they wouldn't leave me, or they would come around more often."

4. "If they had listened to me, everything would be all right."

Any irrational thought needs to be clearly identified, analyzed and restated in realistic terms. This is a constant area for monitoring. Do not let inaccurate thinking prevail.

Parents must also refocus their thinking on their own problems, not on the problems of the children. They should not submerge their own problems in preference to those of others or their own children. Only as they focus can they develop fulfilling solutions to their problems and a satisfying lifestyle. Parents might develop or initiate an activity which they have denied over their years of parenting. Parents might learn new ways of relating to each other and their children. They might seek out or renew significant relationships with other parents.

Depression and Suicide

Although suicide and depression are not synonymous, the presence of chronic depression increases the likelihood of suicidal thoughts and attempts. This possibility should be given importance by the helping professional as well as by the family and friends of the depressed person.

In general, the suicidal person is in a disorganized mental and emotional state. They feel helpless, hopeless,, and are looking desperately for assistance. They are usually anxious, confused and hostile. They feel lonely, rejected and think no one cares. Suicidal behavior can best be understood as an expression of severe emotional distress. It may be an attempt to communicate how deeply distressed they really feel and are crying out for help. Often, they want to end their emotional agony, not their life.

There are several factors which can be use to assess the seriousness of a suicidal gesture. These are, for example:

1. The age and sex of the individual. Suicidal communication from men is generally considered more dangerous than from females. The older the person is, the higher the probability of suicidal intention.

2. The mood of the person. If a patient sounds tired, depressed, washed out, and depleted, the suicidal risk is greater than if there is a degree of self control present. Any marked change in mood, even for the better, is a critical sign among depressed individuals. Increased energy may allow the person freedom to complete the act.

3. The history of prior attempts or threats of suicide. If a person has a past history of serious suicide attempts or threats, then the danger or potential risk increases significantly. Research has shown that many people who commit suicide have a history of attempts or threats.

4. The suicide history of the person. If the suicidal history has been chronic over many years, and if the person's life situation changes to an acute threat to one's personal welfare, then suicide potential increases. Chronic depressed patients are not usually seen as dangerously suicidal as these people have been through crises before and developed ways of getting through a new crisis on the basis of past experience. They are poor long-term risk, however.

5. The method of possible self injury. There are many ways a person can take his/her life. If a person is threatening to use any dangerous method such as a gun, hanging or jumping from a high place, he/she must be taken seriously and restrained. Generally speaking, the more blatant the

threat and the more lethal the method, the more dangerous the person should be considered.

6. The specificity of the method to be utilized. The more the intended suicidal patient can specify the likely steps he/she intends to use, the more eminent the danger.

7. The recent loss of a loved one. The death of a loved one, divorce, marital separation, or the moving away of a close friend all can increase the danger of suicide. It is possible that even the pending loss of a loved one can increase suicidal risk.

8. The presence of physical or medical symptoms. Suicidal risk increases following the onset of physical problems, such as unsuccessful surgery, chronic disability, and learning of the possibility of a life threatening disorder, such as cancer. It also increases among individuals who suffer with chronic sleeplessness, fatigue, impotence and other sexual problems and eating disorders. It is especially dangerous among older people who feel that doctors have mistreated them or that no one can help them or want to help them. Suicide potential increases when there is physical suffering and a fear that one can never be well again. Hopelessness is a serious sign to note.

9. The absence of personal resources to the person. Suicidal risk increases when the patient has no money, has few friends, feels alone, has few social contacts, has recently lost a job or has recently moved. The unavailability of relatives, friends, and family to turn to in stressful circumstances increases the suicidal risk. Feeling alone and helpless is also a serious sign to note.

Finally, when responding in order to prevent suicidal attempts from occurring, there are several generally accepted actions that can be recommended. These include the following:
1. Stay with the person. This might need to continue up to 20 hours.

2. Remove any and all dangerous items from the immediate environment and presence of the threatening individual. This includes knives, medication, rope, guns and any other item that might be indicated.

3. Keep talking. Focus on the anger felt towards others, but which probably has not ever been confronted.

4. Do not offer a bed of roses. It is not proper to say, "All is going to be well," "Everything will be better," or "You are going to be just fine." These statements may constitute a false sense of security, a false hope.

5. Get the person in contact with a professional who is trained, experienced and available to provide immediate help and assistance at the time of crisis. Perhaps you could go along for the first appointment. Be supportive and follow up.

6. Keep in contact with the threatening suicidal person over the coming weeks or months. Help build a support system. Help redirect the person towards a more meaningful set of expectations, goals, associations and interpersonal involvements.

The Use of Medication in the Treatment of Depression

Medication is commonly employed in the treatment of depressed patients. This is generally the only or primary approach taken by family physicians and most psychiatrists in providing psychotherapy. In treating depressed patients, the most typical drugs used are the antidepressants. Antidepressant medications are designed to elevate and regulate the autonomic nervous system. They also serve to increase the mood, energy, and the activity level of the patient. This type of medication requires about 10-15 days to build up in the body prior to its real effect being noticed and providing benefit.

Research seems to indicate that about 50% to 60% of the depressed patients who are treated with medication respond favorably to some degree. However, many prefer not to rely upon drugs as a primary treatment approach. Research has indicated that although some are helped with drugs, most are helped by the psychotherapy that is provided along with the medication. Using drugs alone may be seen as a reliance upon a false external support system and creates the possibility of becoming dependent upon these medications. Negative side effects are also sufficient reason for some patients to reject this approach to therapy as the sole or primary method. Others object to the use of drugs due to deeply rooted personal or religious preference to maintain self control at all times. Since drugs are often used for a brief period of time and the patient must eventually learn to live without medication, some patients prefer not to start the use of medication at all since they will need to learn to live without them anyway.

It is possible that the reliance on drugs might indirectly undermine the patient's utilization of his own self control skills in an attempt to cope with depression. The more a patient attributes the solution of problems to various chemical imbalances or biological factors, the more the patient will attribute any improvement to the drugs being utilized. When this is the case, the patient might be discouraged from drawing upon his/her own coping skills in dealing with depression. The fact that there is a relatively high relapse rate with patients who rely upon drugs, as high as 50% in the year following termination of drug treatment, would indicate that drugs might produce a temporary improvement for some people. This might ultimately prevent the person from developing positive self control strategies to solve the immediate depression and prevent its reoccurrence in the future. The more we develop self control strategies, the more we are able to handle similar crises in the future. Patients need to develop problem solving skills as they learn them from psychotherapy and day to day living experiences. This would suggest that the sole use of drugs without psychotherapy, might be counterproductive as self control skills would not be taught or learned.

A brief word might be directed towards the use of alcohol as a means of controlling negative feelings and irrational thoughts. Besides marijuana, alcohol is the most common drug utilized to manage mood states, such as depression. Besides controlling emotions and thoughts, alcohol is often used to combat sleep disturbances, impulsivity, social anxiety, and prevent unpleasant mood changes. Unfortunately, although alcohol use may produce a desired effect, it only deepens the depression and its associated disturbances. This is commonly the basis for more alcohol and drugs to be consumed. The vicious cycle soon becomes a daily reality and addictive. Unfortunately, all that is being done by alcohol abuse is the temporary quick fix to mask depression. The depression will soon inevitably show itself again when the individual no longer has access to a daily supply of alcohol and/or pills. The depression tends to emerge when a patient withdraws from these chemicals for reasons of health, legal sanction, personal pride, or when some angry family member angrily throws all the alcohol and/or pills away in an attempt to stop the abuse.

Several prescriptive medications commonly taken in good faith also have depressing effects, like alcohol. These drugs include tranquilizers, anti-hypertensives, sedatives, sleeping pills, analgesics, the opioid pain suppressants, cortisone, and other drugs. Unfortunately, many physicians prescribe these medications in an attempt to help the patient manage the signs of depression, but only exacerbate the depression. This is particularly noted in the fact that these kinds of drugs, namely the tranquilizing drugs, are designed to depress the autonomic nervous system and thereby increases depression. There is also a high probability that such patients, while following doctor's orders, become inadvertently "hooked" on these medications and then have the additional problem of addiction to solve along with their attempts to resolve the depression itself. Opioid addiction is particularly troublesome and only makes the depression worse and irresolvable. It is therefore essential that all psychotherapy programs be coordinated with the patient's personal physician so that side effects and associated problems do not occur or can be closely monitored. The same applies for marijuana, a dangerous drug, neurologically and emotionally.

Depression and Aging

The brain develops from birth to age 25 at which age it reaches its maximum development. It then levels off from age 25 to age 50 or 60 with a slight increase in level of functioning around age 40 to 45. After age 60, the brain beings a slow decline with the experience of mild cognitive impairment being relatively common. Mild cognitive impairment is the difficulty of memory of minor events such as the name of someone, a number, of where you put your purse or your car keys when you last laid them down. It is also easy to experience slippage of a story or the facts of an event that had taken place that you are trying to recall and repeat to someone. Usually after age 70 to 80, the normal person enters into a stage of dementia where the memory loss is more pronounced and more pervasive. It is more noticeable and interferes with relationships and general level of functioning. After age 80, it is more likely to enter the stage of Alzheimers, particularly for women.

While this may be a general trend, it certainly does not include all people. There are many exceptions to this pattern. This pattern or profile gives a glimpse of the overall pattern of cognitive and intellectual functioning for most people. Those with a history of depression are more prone to dementia, for example. Also, those with dementia are more likely to manifest depression as a primary mood.

It is during these aging years that an individual must utilize all the strategies and ways in which depression and dementia can be stalled in their progression. For example, socialization must increase. Ongoing education must be a regular event. Listening to music and lectures, and attending seminars would be essential. Physical exercise is essential. Working crossword puzzles and jigsaw puzzles, reading, and other challenging activities are strongly recommended. The withdrawal from alcohol and tobacco smoking would be another essential step to prevent the development of depression and dementia. What you do to prevent and treat depression is also what you do to treat and prevent dementia.

Depression and Employment

Depression impairs every component of an employee's work performance. It interferes, for example, with the ability to produce a timely, accurate, creative, and well-conceived work product.

Consider the Facts

Clinical depression has become one of America's most costly illnesses. It ranks among the top 3 work place problems. 3% of total short-term disability days are due to depressive disorders. If left untreated, the cost to the U.S. economy is approximately $45 billion dollars annually in absenteeism, lost productivity, and direct treatment costs. That is approximately $600.00 per depressed worker per year. Over 200 million work days are lost each year due to depression. A study by the Rand Corporation found that depressed patients spend more days in bed than those with diabetes, arthritis, back problems, lung problems, or gastrointestinal disorders. When alcoholism and drug abuse is involved, especially marijuana, costs escalate and work performance further depreciates. Depression saps the most precious skills a worker brings to the work place - concentration, decision making, judgment, creativity, energy, and concentration, to name a few. The age group most vulnerable to depression is those in the prime working years, age 24 to 44.

What Managers Need to Know

If an employee becomes imperiled by depression, immediately take constructive and restorative action guided by the American Disabilities Act. Time off, flex time, light duty, change of assignment, change of supervisors, reduced time, modifications in work expectations, and assigning a mentor are just of the few options to be considered. It is a goal to keep an employee productive, yet be supportive and assist in overcoming the dark enemy that can rob the work place of a valued employee.

1. Assist the employee to get help. Help the impaired employee draw upon a network of professionals who can assist along the path of recovery to full and productive employment. Be sure the EAP program is utilized. Be sure the mental health insurance plan is fully utilized. Help the employee connect with a local therapist with whom there has been a working relationship or professional respect and confidence.

2. Support the employee while getting help. Support the impaired employee and his or her family in the journey of recovery. Call the spouse. Encourage the family. Offer needed assistance. Be willing to personally visit the employee at critical points in his or her journey of recovery.

3. Be part of the plan for his return to work. Develop a plan for return to employment. Set guidelines. Provide stepping stones. Make it easy to come back and resume one's responsibilities, even if it is undertaken in steps from light duty to full duty, from part-time to full-time employment.

4. Keep the company's benefits up-to-date. Annually review corporate medical, mental health, and EAP programs and benefits. Make sure HR and the EAP representative are trained to make appropriate referrals and provide needed assistance consistent with policies and practices. And, educate employees by reproducing and distributing brochures, pamphlets, and relevant websites. Consider developing a corporate mental health and stress management policy.

What Depressed Employees Need to Know
1. Correct irrational thinking about the job or company. Not all projects and ideas proposed need be approved by management. Further, it is not necessary to be thoroughly competent, adequate, and achieving in all respects of work. It is perfectly acceptable to seek consultation and gather ideas from a variety of sources rather than being the sole source of a proposed plan or idea.

2. Learn to be self-complimentary. When you know you have done a good job or performed well, pause and reflect on a

complimentary phrase about your performance and yourself. Do not be totally dependent upon management and colleagues to compliment you and your performance. While management should be generous in providing complimentary feedback to employees, some managers do not ascribe to such a principle or were not raised in a home in which compliments and affirmation were daily verbal expressions. If a manager or colleague did not learn to affirm others, he or she will not affirm you, even when you think you deserve it.

3. Seek time with colleagues who are encouraging and are positive in their attitudes and speech. In every work environment, there are people who are encouragers and those who are discouragers. There are those who support and those who depreciate others. Avoid the negative people, or help them change. The prevailing attitude of the work force strongly affects the performance and productivity of a company. The emotional tone of the work place affects every worker's level of creativity, accuracy, and output, as well as their emotional health. A healthy work environment is characterized by general happiness, mutual respect and appreciation for colleagues, and agreement with the purpose and mission for which a company is in business.

4. You have the right to assertive communication patterns. Rather than being passive and absorb unwanted and unpleasant communications from others, it is essential that you express your feelings, desires, needs, and preferences. There are times to say "no" and times to say "yes." There are times to ask for help. Learn to get from others what you need and want. Control the degree to which other people overpower or try to control you. Engage in assertive communication so others can better understand you and respond to your needs in a more satisfying manner. Speak up and stop undesirable and unwanted behavior patterns, gestures, verbal expressions, and other innuendoes that create feelings of depression, anxiety, and distress.

5. When faced with a major problem or burdensome task, undertake the problem solving process one step at a time. Be success oriented. Identify the steps that need to be undertaken to

accomplish the task. Start from the known and proceed to the unknown. Start with the simple steps and proceed to the more complex steps. Seek out and accept help from colleagues and management, as needed. Remember, you are not alone. There are others who are willing and able to join in with you so success and accomplishment is achieved in a timely manner.

CONCLUSION

No one should ignore the early warning signs of depression. They are there staring us in the face. Our own depression is most haunting. The depression of others is most distressing. It is all around us – at home, at school, at work, at church, and in our neighborhoods. Depression affects about 10 – 15% of the population. The most vulnerable age group is 24 – 44, more women than men. Helplessness is prevalent.

Treatment is overlooked by many, unfortunately. They pay a great cost in disability, lost productivity, and interpersonal distress in all areas of their lives. By doing nothing, their family pays a great price through dysfunctional living.

Treatment, on the other hand, is sought out by few – the fortunate few. Most reap the benefits of recovery and return to full functioning. The good news is that 80% of those who seek treatment experience recovery – they come out of the darkness. Research indicates that the most effective treatment is a systematic course of psychotherapy along with the use of medication. The coordination of treatment between the therapist and the physician is a winning combination, in most cases.

It is not a matter of coping with depression, but changing it by changing lifestyle, modifying life's circumstances, improving social relationships, engaging in spiritual reflection, learning new behavior patterns, and removing from your life those self-destructive stressors. When such changes are made and treatment is initiated, using self-directed methods and professional consultation, the result will more than likely be positive and satisfying once again.

It is vital that the easy path of alcohol and drugs, especially marijuana, are not the choice of self medication. Only further depression and self-defeating behavior results from such a choice. Self medication is not the answer although it looks tempting to many. The end thereof is only further defeat and destruction. The positive options expressed above are available and the best choice in the long run.

My best to you. . . Keep the faith utmost!

REFERENCES

ALBERTI, E.R., & EMMONS, M.L. *Assert Yourself: It's Your Perfect Right.* San Luis Obispo, CA: Impact Books, 1975

BECK, A., RUSH, A.J., SHOW, B., & EMERY, G. *Cognitive Therapy of Depression.* New York: The Guilford Press, 1979

BENSON, H. The Relaxation Response. New York: Avon, 1975

DYER, WAYNE. *Your Erroneous Zones.* New York: Avon Books, 1976

ELLIS, A. & HARPER, R.A. *A New Guide to Rational Living.* Englewood Cliffs, New Jersey: Prentice Hall, 1975

FARBEROW, N.L. & SHNEIDMAN, E.S. *Cry For Help.* New York: McGraw-Hill, 1961

FERNSTERHEIM, H. & BAER, J. *Don't Say Yes When You Want to Say No.* New York: Den Publishing Co., 1975

GAMBRIL, A.D., & RICHEY, C. *A Social Interaction Manual: Development of Assertive Skills.* Millbrae, Cal: Les Femmes, Celestial Arts, 1976

HAUCK, P. *Overcoming Depression.* Philadelphia: Westminister Press, 1974

HEDBERG, A. *Doctor, Teach Me to Parent,* Bloomington, AuthorHouse, 2013

HEDBERG, A. *Living Life @ its Best,* Bloomington, AuthorHouse, 2013

HEDBERG, A. *Achieving and Living a Healthy Lifestyle: In a World of Stress.* Bloomington, AuthorHouse, 2012

LAKEIN, A. *How to Get Control of Your Time and Your Life.* New Jersey:
New American Library, 1974

OLIVER, ROSE. The Empty Nest Syndrome vs. The Empty Woman. New York: *Psychotherapy: Theory, Research and Practice,* 1977, 14, 87-94

PHELPS S., & AUSTIN N. *The Assertive Woman.* San Luis Obispo, CA : Impact Press, 1975

PIAGET, J. *The Moral Judgment of the Child.* Glencoe, IL: Free Press, 1960

SELIGMAN, M.E.P. *Helplessness.* San Francisco: Freeman, 1975

SELIGMAN, M.E.P. Fall into Helplessness. *Psychology Today.* June, 1973, 43-48

SMITH, J.J. *When I Say No, I Feel Guilty.* New York: Bantam Books, 1975

STRAYHORN, J.M. *Talking It Out: A Guide To Effective Communication and Problem Solving.* Campaign, IL : Research Press Co., 1979

ZUCKERMAN, M., LUBIN, B., VOGEL, L., & VALERIUS, E. Measurement of Experimentally Induced Affects. *J. Consulting Psychology.* 1964, 28, 418-425

ABOUT THE AUTHOR

Dr. Allan G. Hedberg is a clinical psychologist, licensed in the State of California, and maintains a private practice in Fresno. He also serves as a consultant to schools, businesses, hospitals, and many community social agencies. Dr. Hedberg hosts a weekly online TV series, entitled, *Doctor, Teach Me to Parent* on CentralValleyTalk.Com. He also hosts a pod cast for the general public three times weekly - *thepsychologyreport.buzzsprout.com* Dr. Hedberg and his wife, Bernice, live in Fresno and are the parents of three adult children who are all successful in their sphere of living and influence. The cover sketch was drawn by Rob Carey, an internationally acclaimed artist from Clovis, CA. The tree was sketched on location in Wollbach, Germany.

BOOKS BY HEDBERG: Six of the most recent books authored by Dr. Allan Hedberg are available from the office of Dr. Hedberg (559-244-3260) or they can be purchased by accessing his web site, www.booksbyhedberg.com/ They are also available online from Amazon and Barnes and Noble.

The books are:
- *Doctor, Teach me to Parent* … Great book for parents and grandparents.
- *Lessons from my Father*…Lessons we learn from our fathers, or should have learned.
- *Living Life @ its Best* … Lessons in Social Intelligence from Biblical characters.
- *Achieving a Healthy Lifestyle in a* World of Stress … How to live a health life and defeat the ill-affects of stress.
- *Jonathan Edwards: A Life Well Lived* … Learning from the greatest American pastor ever to lead the church.
- *Kids Alive . . .* Helping parents teach important values and behavior patterns to their young children.

OUT OF THE DARKNESS OF DEPRESSION: Positive Strategies to Guide You will provide a basic understanding of depression and will be a helpful guide to those desiring to prevent depression or overcome it in their lives. It will be of help to depressed individuals, parents of depressed children, families with a history of depression, and professional therapists.